# 12 REASONS TO LOVE
# **SKIING AND**
# **SNOWBOARDING**

by Joanne Mattern

STORY LIBRARY
MORE TO EXPLORE

12-Story Library is an imprint of Amicus.

Developed and produced for 12-Story Library by Focus Strategic Communications Inc.

**Library of Congress Cataloging-in-Publication Data**
Names: Mattern, Joanne, 1963- author.
Title: 12 reasons to love skiing and snowboarding / by Joanne Mattern.
Other titles: Twelve reasons to love skiing and snowboarding
Description: Mankato, Minnesota : 12-Story Library, 2020. | Series: Sports report | Includes
  bibliographical references and index. | Audience: Ages 10–13 | Audience: Grades 4–6
Identifiers: LCCN 2020014888 (print) | LCCN 2020014889 (ebook) | ISBN 9781645821304
  (library binding) | ISBN 9781645821687 (paperback) | ISBN 9781645822059 (pdf)
Subjects: LCSH: Skis and skiing—Juvenile literature. | Snowboarding—Juvenile literature.
Classification: LCC GV854.315 .M37 2020 (print) | LCC GV854.315 (ebook) | DDC 796.93—dc23
LC record available at https://lccn.loc.gov/2020014888
LC ebook record available at https://lccn.loc.gov/2020014889

Photographs ©: Artur Didyk/Shutterstock.com, cover, 1; Ian Bottle/Alamy, 4; Art Collection 3/
Alamy, 5; PD, 5; Glasshouse Images/Alamy, 5; erin mcdaniel/YouTube.com, 6; azbikerider49/
YouTube.com, 6; PA Images/Alamy, 7; sportpoint/Shutterstock.com, 7; imageBROKER/Alamy, 8;
shopics/Alamy, 9; Macromomy/Alamy, 9; Ivan Feoktistov/Shutterstock.com, 9; StockphotoVideo/
Shutterstock.com, 10; imageBROKER/Alamy, 11; mountainpix/Shutterstock.com, 11; Michael
Grubka/Alamy, 12; Artie Medvedev/Shutterstock.com, 13; Chuck Franklin/Alamy, 13; MWiklik/
Shutterstock.com, 14; Ivan Smuk/Alamy, 15; PSI-AASI/YouTube.com, 15; gorillaimages/
Shutterstock.com, 16; Elizaveta Galitckaia/Shutterstock.com, 17; CBS/YouTube.com, 17; ÖNB/
Willinger, W., 18; Rob Crandall/Shutterstock.com, 19; Today News/YouTube.com, 19; Jonas
Ericcsoon/CC4.0, 20; Action Plus Sports Images/Alamy, 21; Jaroslav Moravcik/Shutterstock.com,
21; roger tillberg/Alamy, 22; Mitch Gunn/Shutterstock.com, 22; PHOTOMDP/Shutterstock.com, 23;
Ken Blaze/Alamy, 23; Keystone Press/Alamy, 24; PA Images/Alamy, 24; dpa picture alliance/Alamy,
25; PA Images/Alamy, 25; Mike Dotta/Shutterstock.com, 26; Martynova Anna/Shutterstock.com,
27; dpa picture alliance/Alamy, 27; dpa picture alliance/Alamy, 27; Marcin Kadziolka/
Shutterstock.com, 28; CandyBox Images/Shutterstock.com, 29; iofoto/Shutterstock.com, 29;
melissamn/Shutterstock.com, 29

Printed in the United States of America
HC   10 9 8 7 6 5 4 3 2 1
PB   10 9 8 7 6 5 4 3 2 1

## About the Cover

A skier and snowboarder jumping.

Access free, up-to-date content on this topic plus a full digital version of this book. Scan the QR code on page 31 or use your school's login at **12StoryLibrary.com**.

T 7734

# Table of Contents

# Skiing Is an Ancient Sport

Old skis from Norway displayed at a museum.

that had lots of winter weather.

Scientists have found cave paintings that show people using skis. They have also found ancient skis preserved in wet places called bogs. Norse mythology even had a god and goddess of skiing, named Ullr and Skade.

Skiing has been around for at least 8,000 years. Even the word *ski* is ancient. It comes from an Old Norse word, *skio*, which meant *long snowshoe* or *long stick of wood*. Using long sticks to glide over the snow was a quick way to get around in places

By about 1,000 years ago, farmers, hunters, and warriors in northern Europe were using skis to get around. Later, soldiers in the Swedish army trained and competed on skis.

Ullr (left) and Skade.

By the 1880s, downhill skiing had become a popular sport. People enjoyed the rush of zooming down a snowy mountain. Skiing became very popular in the Alps.

In 1936, downhill, or alpine, skiing was added to the Winter Olympics.

Kalle Heikkinen competes at the 1936 Olympics in Germany.

# 6300 BCE
## The date of the world's oldest skis

- They were discovered in Russia.
- Rock carvings of a skier in Norway date back to 4000 BCE.
- Around 3300 BCE, skis with grooves were discovered in Finland.

# Snowboarding Started with a New Invention

Sherman Poppen, 2011.

added a rope to the front so he could pull and steer his new toy. Then he and his children stood on the skis and surfed down a snowy hill. Poppen's wife called the new toy the Snurfer.

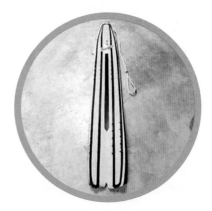

Unlike skiing, snowboarding is a fairly new sport. It was created in 1965. That's when a man named Sherman Poppen came up with a new idea for his children's Christmas present.

Poppen fastened two skis together. He

In 1972, Dimitrije Milovich created the modern snowboard. He founded a company called Winterstick. Later, other inventors started their own companies.

Many ski resorts did not like snowboarding. But as

Yuri Yoshikawa competes at the 1998 Olympics in Nagano, Japan.

the sport became more popular, most ski areas allowed snowboarders on their hills. In 1998, snowboarding became an Olympic sport.

## THINK ABOUT IT

Why do you think ski areas did not welcome snowboarders? Why did they change their minds?

# 1982

### Year the first major snowboarding competition was held

- The contest was held at Vermont's Suicide Six ski resort.
- Snowboarders traveled at more than 50 miles per hour (80 kph).
- Hay bales were used as crash pads during the event.

**3**

# Equipment
# Is High Tech

Wooden skis
around 1937.

When it comes to skis and
snowboards, things have
changed a lot over the years.
Today's skis and boards are
super high tech.

Skis were mostly made of
wood. That changed in 1947.
Inventors discovered
that aluminum skis

were stronger and
easier to maneuver.
In 1959, fiberglass skis were
invented. That made skis
lighter and easier to turn.

Like skis, snowboards were
originally made of wood. Then
they changed to metal, plastic,
and fiberglass. Inventors

created wider boards. Today, boards come in different shapes and sizes. They let snowboarders be as creative as they want to.

Traditional Camber

Reverse Camber &Rocker

Flat Camber

Camber Combination

# 1997
**Year Mike Douglas invented the twin-tip ski**

- Twin-tip skis have the same shape of tip at both ends of the ski.
- The shape allows skiers to jump, ski, and land backward.
- Douglas wanted skiers to be able to do the same tricks snowboarders could.

## CAMBER VS. ROCKER

Skis and snowboards have two basic shapes. Cambered skis and boards have an arch in the middle. Rockers are flat in the middle and curved upward on the ends. Cambers are better on hard snow. Rockers help athletes float and turn on soft snow.

# There Are Different Kinds of Skiing

Mischa Gasser performs aerial skiing during a competition in Ukraine in 2013.

Skiing is not just zooming down a snowy hill. There are several different types of skiing.

Alpine skiing is also called downhill skiing. This style gets its name from the Alps mountains in Switzerland. Alpine skiers usually take a lift to the top of a mountain and ski down. This is the most popular type of skiing.

10

Telemark skiing is like alpine skiing, with one big difference. In alpine skiing, the heels of the skier's boots are attached to the skis. In telemark, the heels are not attached. This lets the skier be more flexible.

Telemark ski and boot.

Freestyle skiers do turns and tricks in the air. One popular type of freestyle skiing involves moguls. Mogul skiers navigate a course that includes large bumps.

Aerial skiers take off from a ski jump. They perform different flips and twists in the air. Then they land on the slope and ski to the bottom.

A freestyle skier performing a high jump.

## 394

**Height in feet (120 m) of the Olympic ski jump**

- The height has been the same since the 1992 Games.
- Athletes get two jumps.
- They are scored on the distance of the jump and their style.

# Snow Sports Use a Lot of Equipment

Skis and snowboards are just the start of the necessary equipment for these sports. Many skiers also use poles. Poles help skiers balance. They also allow skiers to turn better at high speeds. If a skier gets stuck, the poles can help push him out of trouble.

Bindings link the athlete's feet to the skis or snowboard. They are also a safety feature. Bindings release the athlete's feet in case of a fall or other accident.

Both skiers and snowboarders need to wear the right clothes. Jackets, snow pants, gloves, and socks protect athletes from the cold and the wind. Goggles protect their eyes from the wind and the snow.

Ski bindings.

# $800

**Average cost of new skis, boots, and bindings**

- Custom skis can cost $1,000 or more.
- Lift tickets can also cost up to $150 at some areas.
- Casual skiers rent equipment at $20 to $50 a day to save money.

They also protect from the glare of the sun on the snow.

All skiers and snowboarders should wear helmets.

Even the best athletes will fall, and helmets are vital to protect against head injuries.

# 6

# Snow Makes a Difference

Not all snow is created equal. The type of snow affects the way skis and snowboards travel.

Powder is the best snow for skiing. This snow has just fallen and is soft and smooth.

After lots of people ski over powder, it becomes crunchy. This type of snow is called *crud*. Even worse is when the top layer melts and refreezes into a crust.

If snow melts and doesn't refreeze, it turns into slush.

Real powder snow is ideal for skiing.

## REAL VS. ARTIFICIAL

Ski areas make artificial snow by spraying a mist of water high in the air so that ice crystals form. But skiers like the real thing better. Real snow is usually drier and easier to move on.

Slush is wet and heavy. Skis don't slide over it very well.

The worst surface to ski on is ice. Ice occurs when all the layers of snow melt and refreeze. Ice is hard and slippery.

## 51
### Number of ski areas in New York State in 2018–2019

- New York has more ski areas than any other state.
- Michigan is second, with 43 areas.
- A few southern states have ski areas, too.

It's difficult to ski on ice.

# Skiing Is for All Ages

Almost any age is a good age to hit the slopes. Most teachers say children as young as three can learn to ski. At this age, lessons focus on getting used to the equipment and gliding on very low hills.

Snowboarding lessons can start around 5 years old. Younger children may have trouble balancing on a snowboard. Like skiing, snowboard lessons for children are more about getting comfortable on the board than conquering huge hills.

Adults of just about any age can ski or snowboard.

Snowboarding can be fun for young kids.

## THINK ABOUT IT

Do you think there should be an age when a person is "too old" to ski or snowboard? Why or why not?

Although most snowboarders are younger than 35, others continue snowboarding in their 40s, 50s, and beyond. And some people ski all their lives, even at over 100.

# 107

**Age of Lou Batori when he skied for the last time, shortly before he died in 2018.**

- Batori started skiing when he was 10 years old.
- He was born in Hungary but grew up in the US.
- In 2018, Crystal Mountain Ski Area in Michigan named a run after Batori.

# 8

# You Can Hit the Slopes Indoors

The first indoor slope was only about 60 feet (18 m) high.

It sounds weird, but there are several places where you can ski and snowboard indoors.

The world's first indoor ski hall opened in Vienna, Austria, in 1927. The slope was inside an empty train station. The "snow" was made of chemicals and soda.

Today's indoor ski areas are much bigger and fancier. Ski Dubai opened in the United Arab Emirates in 2005. The temperature inside is always below zero.

Ski Dubai.

That's quite a difference from the hot weather in the desert outside.

In December 2019, the first indoor ski area in the United States opened in New Jersey. Big Snow American Dream is a huge ski and snowboard park. The area has both easy and difficult trails.

# 160
**The drop in feet (49 m) of the ski hill at Big Snow American Dream.**

- Big Snow has four acres of trails.
- The center can make 1,100 gallons (4,200 l) of snow per hour.
- The average depth of snow is two feet (60 cm).

## AN EVEN BIGGER CENTER?

A park called Wintastar Shanghai is being built in China. It is expected to cover one million square feet (93,000 m²).

# Competitions Are Exciting

Marcel Hirscher competes at the FIS alpine ski world championship in St. Moritz, 2017.

There are many exciting competitions in skiing and snowboarding. For skiing, the World Cup is the top. This event has been held every year since 1967. It is sponsored by the Federation Internationale de Ski, or FIS. Athletes compete in events around the world.

The man and woman who receive the most points are the champions.

World Cup slopes are not for the average skier. Slopes are very high and steep. Jumps are huge. Skiers can achieve speeds of more than 80 miles per hour (130 kph) as they zoom down these extreme tracks.

Sometimes even the most experienced skiers can fall on these dangerous slopes.

For snowboarders, the Winter X Games are an exciting competition. Sponsored by ESPN, a television sports network, these games focus on extreme sports. (The X stands for *extreme*.) Snowboarders can also compete in US Open Events. There is also a World Cup championship, sponsored by the FIS.

## THINK ABOUT IT

What qualities are important for champion skiers and snowboarders to have?

# 1910
**Year the FIS was founded**

- Twenty-two members from 10 countries attended the first meeting.
- Today, the FIS includes 132 ski associations from around the world.
- The FIS sets the rules for all international competitions in skiing.

# Skiing Has Great Athletes

Ingemar Stenmark has the best record of all time for a male skier. This Swedish alpine skier dominated during the 1970s. He won a record 86 World Cup titles. He also won two Olympic gold medals in 1980.

Lindsey Vonn is the greatest female skier. She has a record 82 World Cup victories. She was the first American woman to win a gold medal in downhill skiing at the 2010 Olympics.

Here's a look at the best of the best athletes on the slopes.

Lindsey Vonn, 2009.

Bode
Miller 2013.

Bode Miller is the most successful male American World Cup winner of all time. Miller has won 33 World Cup races. He is one of only five men to win World Cup events in all five areas.

## AS FAST AS POSSIBLE

Bode Miller once said he wants to ski as fast as the universe allows.

# 13

## Age of snowboarder Shaun White when he turned pro in 1996

- White was 16 when he became the youngest snowboarder to win the US Open.
- He also competes in skateboarding.
- He is the only athlete to win gold at both the winter and summer X Games.

23

# Olympic Moments Are Highlights

Skiers and snowboarders have created amazing Olympic moments since the Winter Games began in 1924. In 1968, French skier Jean-Claude Killy won all the alpine skiing events. He had already won two World Cups.

Croatia's Janica Kostelić is one of the top women's skiers at the Olympics. She won four gold medals and two silver medals at the 1998 and 2002 Olympics. Kostelić said the more difficult the conditions, the better she skied.

Janica Kostelić, Salt Lake City, 2002.

Jamie Anderson, South Korea, 2018.

Shaun White is the best-known Olympic snowboarder. But he isn't the only great athlete in this sport. Fellow American Jamie Anderson has won two golds and a silver medal in women's snowboarding events.

Jenny Jones is the most successful British snowboarder. She won a bronze medal at the 2014 Olympics. That made her the first British athlete to ever medal in a snow sport.

## 2

**Number of gold medals won by Hermann Maier after a horrifying crash at the 1998 Olympics**

- The accident happened 17 seconds into the downhill race.
- In 2001, Maier was in a bad motorcycle crash, yet he still won a silver and bronze medal in the 2006 Olympics.
- Maier retired in 2009.

Jenny Jones, 2014.

25

# Skiing and Snowboarding Are Adaptive Sports

Anyone who wants to ski or snowboard should have the chance to do so. This is true even if the athlete is disabled. There are many opportunities for athletes of all abilities to ski, snowboard, and compete.

Adaptive skiers and snowboarders use special equipment. Some skiers use extra skis and poles to help them balance. Others use a mono-ski or bi-ski. These include seats mounted on one or two wide skis. This seat helps athletes who cannot walk or stand. Blind athletes can ski with a guide.

Adaptive snowboarding is a fairly new sport. Some athletes use

The Paralympic Games were started to provide athletic competition for injured veterans of World War II. These Games feature events in many different sports, for athletes with many different physical and mental challenges.

special bindings to keep their balance. Others use prosthetic feet. Almost anything is possible in adaptive sports.

# 19
## Age of Amy Purdy when she had both legs amputated

- Two years later, she won three medals at the USASA National Snowboarding Championship.
- Purdy founded an organization to help disabled athletes.
- In 2014, she was the only double amputee to compete in the Sochi Paralympics.

- In 2006, Simone Origone set a world speed skiing record of 156.2 miles per hour (251.4 kph).

- Anders Fannemel of Norway holds the world record for the longest ski jump. He jumped just over 825 feet (251 m) in 2015.

- Knee and leg injuries are the most common injuries in skiing. Other snowboarding injuries include shoulder and upper arm damage.

- Snowboarding made its first Olympic appearance in 1998. Ross Rebagliati of Canada won the first snowboarding gold medal.

- Ski slopes are rated by how difficult they are. Trails for beginners are marked with a green circle. Intermediate trails have a blue square. Difficult slopes are marked with a black diamond. A double black diamond means the slope is extremely difficult and dangerous.

# Glossary

**adaptive**
Something, such as equipment, that is changed to help people use it.

**aerial**
Taking place in the air, such as sports like ski jumping.

**amputate**
Cut off a limb for medical reasons.

**ancient**
From a very long time ago.

**association**
A group of people who work together for a shared purpose.

**custom**
Something that is made to order especially for an individual or group.

**dominate**
Do much better than anyone else in a competition and outshine all rivals.

**extreme**
Sporting activities that are dangerous and involve the risk of injury.

**flexible**
Athletes or performers are able to bend their bodies easily without breaking.

**lift**
Chairs on a cable that carry skiers up a mountain.

**prosthetic**
An artificial body part such as an arm or foot that replaces something missing.

**sponsor**
A person or organization that support a an activity by giving money or products or other help.

# Read More

Hamilton, John. *Snowboarding*. Minneapolis, MN: Abdo Publishing Company, 2015.

Hewson, Anthony K. *Shaun White*. Minneapolis, MN: Abdo Publishing, 2019.

Trusdell, Brian. *Great Moments in Olympic Skiing*. Minneapolis, MN: Abdo Publishing Company, 2015.

Turnbull, Stephanie. *Skiing and Snowboarding*. Mankato, MN: Smart Apple Media, 2016.

## Visit 12StoryLibrary.com

Scan the code or use your school's login at **12StoryLibrary.com** for recent updates about this topic and a full digital version of this book. Enjoy free access to:

- Digital ebook
- Breaking news updates
- Live content feeds
- Videos, interactive maps, and graphics
- Additional web resources

**Note to educators:** Visit 12StoryLibrary.com/register to sign up for free premium website access. Enjoy live content plus a full digital version of every 12-Story Library book you own for every student at your school.

# Index

## About the Author

Joanne Mattern has been writing books for children for more than 25 years. She loves to write about sports. Snowy winters are one of her favorite things. Joanne lives in New York state with her family.